Let's Explore

Saving Money

by Laura Hamilton Waxman

LERNER PUBLICATIONS ◆ MINNEAPOLIS

Note to Educators

Throughout this book, you'll find critical-thinking questions. These can be used to engage young readers in thinking critically about the topic and in using the text and photos to do so.

Lerner Publications Company
A division of Lerner Publishing Group, Inc.
241 First Avenue North
Minneapolis, MN 55401 USA

For reading levels and more information, look up this title at www.lernerbooks.com.

Library of Congress Cataloging-in-Publication Data

Names: Waxman, Laura Hamilton, author.
Title: Let's explore saving money / Laura Hamilton Waxman.
Description: Minneapolis, MN : Lerner Publications, [2019] | Series: Bumba books™ — A first look at money | Audience: Age: 4–7. | Audience: K to Grade 3. | Includes bibliographical references and index.
Identifiers: LCCN 2018011596 (print) | LCCN 2018035237 (ebook) | ISBN 9781541542952 (eb pdf) | ISBN 9781541538542 (lb : alk. paper)
Subjects: LCSH: Saving and investment—Juvenile literature. | Shopping—Juvenile literature.
Classification: LCC HB822 (ebook) | LCC HB822 .W39 2019 (print) | DDC 332.024—dc23

LC record available at https://lccn.loc.gov/2018011596

Manufactured in the United States of America
1-45037-35864-5/30/2018

Table of Contents

Saving Your Money

People use money to buy many things.

Food and clothes cost money.

Toys cost money too.

BLACKBERRIES $4 EA

STRAWBERRIES $3 EA

BLUEBERRIES — $5 EA

RASPBERRIES — $5 EA

5

Sometimes things cost more

money than you have.

What can you do?

You can start saving.

That means you don't spend your money.

You keep it until you have enough.

Has anyone ever given you money?

You can save it.

Do you do chores to earn money?

You can save it.

What are some other ways to earn money?

Families save money too.

They might save to buy a car.

They might save for a place

to live.

Many families save money

in a bank.

They take money out when

they need it.

You can save your money in a jar.

You can save it in a piggy bank.

Where else can you save your money?

You can use your saved money to buy things.

Then you can start saving again!

Why Save Money?

The pictures below show things that cost money. Point to the things families might need to save for. Then point to what you might like to save for.

Picture Glossary

earn

to make money by selling something or doing work

money

bills and coins used to buy things

save

to put away your money and not use it

spend

to use money to buy things you need or want

Read More

Bullard, Lisa. *Shanti Saves Her Money*. Minneapolis: Millbrook Press, 2014.

Higgins, Nadia. *Saving Money*. Minneapolis: Jump!, 2018.

Shoulders, Debbie. *M Is for Money: An Economics Alphabet*. Ann Arbor, MI: Sleeping Bear, 2015.

Index

Photo Credits

Image credits: Amy Salveson/Independent Picture Service (piggy bank icons throughout); Maria Nuzzo/ EyeEm/Getty Images, p. 5; Jamie Grill/Getty Images, pp. 6–7; MPIX/Shutterstock.com, pp. 8, 23 (bottom left); KidStock/Blend Images/Getty Images, p. 10; granata68/Shutterstock.com, pp. 13, 23 (top left); monkeybusinessimages/iStock/Getty Images, pp. 14–15; Jim Cummins/The Image Bank/Getty Images, p. 17; Jason Kolenda/Shutterstock.com, p. 18; Inti St Clair/Blend Images/Getty Images, pp. 21, 23 (bottom right); AlexLinck/Shutterstock.com, p. 22 (house); Peter Vanco/Shutterstock.com, p. 22 (toy elephant); tobkatrina/Shutterstock.com, p. 22 (soccer ball); OlgaGi/Shutterstock.com, p. 22 (boots); Ed Aldridge/ Shutterstock.com, p. 22 (car); Todd Strand/Independent Picture Service, p. 23 (top right).

Cover: r.classen/Shutterstock.com.